ask the kabala
oracle cards guidebook

DEEPAK CHOPRA
& MICHAEL "ZAPPY" ZAPOLIN
with Alys R. Yablon

Carlsbad, California
London • Sydney • Johannesburg
Vancouver • Hong Kong • Mumbai

Copyright © 2006 by Deepak Chopra, Michael Zapolin, and Alys R. Yablon

Published and distributed in the United States by: Hay House, Inc.: www.hayhouse.com • ***Published and distributed in Australia by:*** Hay House Australia Pty. Ltd.: www.hayhouse.com.au • ***Published and distributed in the United Kingdom by:*** Hay House UK, Ltd.: www.hayhouse.co.uk • ***Published and distributed in the Republic of South Africa by:*** Hay House SA (Pty), Ltd.: orders@psdprom.co.za • ***Distributed in Canada by:*** Raincoast: www.raincoast.com • ***Published in India by:*** Hay House Publications (India) Pvt. Ltd.: www.hayhouseindia.co.in • ***Distributed in India by:*** Media Star: booksdivision@mediastar.co.in

Editorial supervision: Jill Kramer • *Design:* Charles McStravick
Interior illustrations: Tracy Walker

All rights reserved. No part of this guidebook may be reproduced by any mechanical, photographic, or electronic process, or in the form of a phonographic recording; nor may it be stored in a retrieval system, transmitted, or otherwise be copied for public or private use—other than for "fair use" as brief quotations embodied in articles and reviews without prior written permission of the publisher. The intent of the authors is only to offer information of a general nature to help you in your quest for emotional and spiritual well-being. In the event you use any of the information in this book for yourself, which is your constitutional right, the authors and the publisher assume no responsibility for your actions.

Printed in China by Imago

Contents

PART I: OVERVIEW

Introduction by Deepak Chopra vii
How to Use This Booklet xix
Chapter 1: A Brief History of Kabala 3
Chapter 2: The Mysteries of the Aleph-Bet . . . 11

PART II: THE LETTER CARDS

1. Aleph: *Avram* (Abraham) 25
2. Bet: *Migdal Bavel* (Tower of Babel) 29
3. Gimmel: *Ger* (The Stranger) 34
4. Dalet: *LeDavek* (To Cleave) 38
5. Heh: *Hinneni* ("Here I Am") 44
6. Vav: *Vidui* (Confession) 49
7. Zayin: *Zachor et Yom HaShabbat*
   (Remember the Sabbath Day) 53

8	Chet: *Challah*	58
9	Tet: *Tov* (Goodness)	62
10	Yud: *Yosef* (Joseph)	66
11	Caph: *Calev* (Caleb)	72
12	Lamed: *Leah*	77
13	Mem: *Miriam*	83
14	Nun: *Noach* (Noah)	88
15	Samech: *Har Sinai* (Mount Sinai)	93
16	Ayin: *Akedat Yitzchak* (The Binding of Isaac)	98
17	Peh: *Pharoah*	104
18	Tzaddik: *Tzelem Elohim* (Image of God)	109
19	Kuf: *Kan-Tzippor* (Bird's Nest)	114
20	Resh: *Rivka* (Rebecca)	118
21	Shin: *Shema Yisrael* (Hear, O Israel)	123
22	Tav: *Tohu U'Vohu* (Vast Nothingness)	127

Bibliography 133

About the Authors 137

PART I

Overview

Introduction
BY DEEPAK CHOPRA

My spiritual background is in the Vedic tradition—the knowledge of the great Seers of India, which has been expressed in a body of ancient literature known as the Upanishads. More than two decades ago, I became aware of the similarities between Vedic Cognition (the knowledge of a higher order) and Judaic Cognition, expressed mainly in the study of Kabala. (Please note that for the sake of clarity, all Kabala terms in this booklet are in italics, while Vedic terms are not.)

The parallel concepts in these two traditions are uncanny and vast. To name just a few: the Universal Domain or Infinite Source of life referred to as Brahman in Vedic tradition is known as the realm of *Ein Sof* (literally, "without end") in Judaism; the Wandering Atman of my tradition is called *Gilgul HaNefesh* ("cyclic reincarnation of the wandering soul") in the other; the *Shechina,* the feminine face of God, corresponds to Shakti; and the parallel worlds known as *Olamot* are what I would call Lokas. Similarly, in kabalistic tradition, as in the Vedic, there are corresponding realms of existence ranging from the causal to the subtle to the physical.

How can two such seemingly different traditions exhibit such similar systems of understanding and interpreting the worlds around and within us?

One way of understanding this is to go back as far as the period between 2000 and 3000 B.C., which many historians call the Axial Age. During this period there appeared on our planet the prophets of the Old Testament in the Middle East; the sages of the Upanishads in India; Greek philosophers such as Socrates, Plato, Parmenides, and Pythagoras; and great Seers such as Lao-Tzu and Confucius in the Far East. Buddha, who predated Christ by about 500 years, can also be included in this category—as, of course, can Jesus Christ himself.

The Axial Age is thus called because the same incredible phenomenon occurred all around the earth within approximately the same time frame: A handful of luminaries worldwide brought the concept of self-awareness to humanity. Although their vocabularies represent the languages of their particular places and times, their contributions to our understanding of the world are incredibly similar. If we were to summarize the insights of these great Seers, we'd be able to say that they saw three levels of existence in the universe: the Physical, the Mental, and the Spiritual.

The Domains of the Physical, Mental, and Spiritual Worlds

The **Physical Domain** of existence is the one we experience through our five senses. It's three-dimensional and consistently changing, and in it cause and effect seem to be fixed. Every organism that's born eventually dies and is subject to decay. Objects appear to have firm boundaries, and events seem to be definite. Matter dominates over energy, and the laws of nature seem to be predictable.

Kabalists refer to this domain as the "one percent world" because it's a very small fragment of a much larger, invisible realm referred to as the "ninety-nine percent world." Today, science informs us that the visible universe is in fact less than one-billionth of the invisible level of existence.

The second level of existence is one that the great Seers of the Wisdom traditions recognized as the **Mental Domain**—that of thoughts, feelings, emotions, dreams, fantasies, memories, and desires. We experience this world as our personal subjectivity.

The third level of existence, the **Spiritual Domain**, was felt to be beyond the mental. According to the great Seers, this state of being is our connection to the Creator or God, an immortal domain beyond birth or death, the source of both the Mental and Physical domains.

Frequently, the Physical Domain, the "one percent world" of the Kabala, is called the Biosphere when referring to living organisms (plants and animals), and the Geosphere when referring to nonliving physical matter such as rocks. The Mental Domain is often called the Noosphere, and the Spiritual Domain is known as the Theosphere.

Many contemporary, cutting-edge scientists feel that the distinction between mind and matter may be merely a matter of convenience and, therefore, arbitrary. According to some theorists, our planet is a living organism with a biology, just like any other creature. Furthermore, since all living creatures have a subjective realm of existence, it's maintained that our earth, being alive, is imbued with subjectivity and creativity.

Other scientists have suggested that photons are the carriers of both subjective and objective information in the universe, and since the whole universe is permeated by photons, it's a conscious being. According to this theory, what we refer to as the Quantum Domain of Nature is actually the "mind field" of nature: the world of information and energy. It's at this level that creation manifests. Here, cause and effect are fluid, and both life and death occur in the speed of light. At this level information is embedded in energy, everything is indivisible and oscillating, and we're all connected through networks of information and energy. Our thoughts are the thoughts of nature, and our energy is part of the energy fields of nature.

The Theosphere: Personal, Collective, and Universal Domains

The third level of existence is referred to as the Theosphere, the realm of the Divine. This level has more depth than the other two and is compartmentalized into a Personal Domain (the level of the soul); a Collective Domain (the level of archetypes); and a Universal Domain, which is the immeasurable potential of all that was, all that is, and all that is to come.

The Theosphere is immortal, beyond birth and death. Here, everything is correlated with everything else simultaneously. It is silent, eternal, and the source of all energy and information; it also has infinite organizing power and infinite creative potential, and is immeasurable and dynamic.

Our senses give us the experience of linear time and cause/effect relationships. As a result, we also think in those terms. The *real* reality, however, is that life and the universe function with **simultaneity and correlation.** How else could a human body think thoughts, play a violin, kill germs, remove toxins, harbor emotions, and make a baby all at once . . . *and* correlate these activities with each other instantly?

The human body has approximately one hundred trillion cells—more than all the stars in the Milky Way galaxy. Every cell is performing millions of activities every second, and all cells instantly correlate their activities with all the other cells—without the exchange of energy or information signals. This is the realm of omniscience, omnipresence, and the omnipotent. Our personal and collective soul belongs to this infinite domain.

The Swiss psychologist Carl Jung referred to the archetypal level of the Theosphere as the "collective unconscious." Although Jung had great insights into the nature of the submanifest order of being, I think the term "unconscious" is inaccurate. Instead, I refer to the domain of archetypes in the Theosphere as the domain of nonlocal awareness, which is much more alert than our limited ego mind. When we tap into this domain, we experience insight, intuition, creative imagination, inspiration, and conscious choice-making. Here we also realize the full potential of the power of intention.

The realm of archetypes, angels, and higher beings is known as *Atzilut* in the Kabala, and Ananda Maya Kosa in Vedic literature. The realm of the subtle body and seeds of personal identity is *Beriya* (Gyan Maya Kosa), and the realm of emotions is *Yetzira* (Mano Maya Kosa). The physical domain, the realm of space, time, and causality, is *Assiya* (Anna Maya Kosa).

Beriya differentiates as *Chochma*, *Bina*, and *Da'at*. These are correspondingly the creative impulse, nurturing impulse, and integrating impulse in the Noosphere; and Mahat, Ego, and Beliefs in the world of Gyan Maya Kosa.

Yetzira differentiates into *Hessed*, *Geruvah*, and *Tiferet*. These are internalized emotions that express themselves as correspondingly giving and receiving, restraint, forbearance, and focused energy (Sattva, Tamas, and Rajas in the Vedic tradition). The externalized emotions are *Netzach*, *Hod*, and *Yesod*, which express themselves correspondingly as reaching out, compassion, empathic listening, understanding, sacred communion, love, and bonding (parallel to karmically appropriate action, Shruti, and the cosmic embrace of Shiva and Shakti, respectively).

Correspondingly, *Assiya* in the physical domain expresses the actualization of latent tendencies through behavior and action, as in Karma Yoga. This relates to the *Malchut,* which is associated with the *Shechina,* the feminine face of God (Shakti in Vedic tradition).

All these realms of existence, however, are expressions of a single reality: consciousness itself, the ground state of existence. When we use oracles for prophecy or for understanding the deeper realms of existence that give rise to the more manifest realms of existence, we begin to realize how archetypes synchronistically orchestrate events in our personal and collective lives.

Archetypes are concentrations of psychic energy: They're states of information, energy, and awareness in potential. They exist in the collective domain of the Theosphere, manifesting as particular themes or stories or motifs from the virtual to the quantum to the physical domains. An archetype exists as potential, and it lies dormant until triggered by some situation in the environment or in the conscious or unconscious mental life of an individual. It can also be consciously triggered through intent.

The activation of an archetype releases patterning forces (states of energy information and awareness) that restructure space-time events, both internally (psychically) and externally (the world of objects, relationships, and circumstances)—as a tangled hierarchy. This restructuring is ordered by the infinite organizing power of the virtual domain and operates outside the laws of space, time, and causality. It orchestrates SynchroDestiny, or the spontaneous fulfillment of desire.

Putting It All Together: The Total Universe

How does this knowledge relate to what you'll discover in *Ask the Kabala*?

Well, we now understand from physics the phenomenon known as the Observer Effect, as described by the eminent physicist John Wheeler. Essentially, this principle states that the universe, at its fundamental core, is a field of possibilities, which is compelled to make choices when asked questions.

Is it wavelike? Yes, if you ask a wavelike question.

Is it particle-like? Yes, if you do a particle-like experiment.

But what is it before you ask the question or do the experiment? Neither. It remains a potential wave and a potential particle, simultaneously.

This means that the observer, the observed, the process of observation, and the question asked at the moment of observation all simultaneously create the space/time event we call Reality. In essence, they're all a single pattern of behavior of the Total Universe.

When you pose a question to the Kabala and get a particular answer—and interpret it in your own personal way—you're doing the same thing. You, the universe, the archetypal patterns you obtain, and how you interpret them, are all a single activity of the Total Universe.

You and I may be asking different or similar questions, and be getting different or similar answers, but the interpretations we bring to them are uniquely ours because we interpret through the filter of our own experience. This experience may be personal (called Personal Karma in Eastern traditions) or it may be part of our spiritual inheritance and that of our ancestors. If you're from the Jewish tradition, for example, and come from a family steeped in the knowledge of Torah, then your interpretations would be very different than those of someone less familiar with this tradition. This doesn't mean, however, that that person's interpretation would be less reliable—just more pertinent to them.

How to Use This Booklet

In the following pages, you'll find short essays corresponding to each of the 22 letters of the Hebrew alphabet. We've chosen just one archetypal theme, story, or character out of many from the Old Testament to represent each letter, but in those stories you'll find many other hidden paths and messages leading you to a deeper understanding of the letters and, ultimately, of yourself. At the end of each essay is a short meditation on the themes expressed in these essays.

To begin, choose a card from the deck included in this package. You should shuffle the cards ahead of time and hold them, facedown, in your left hand. Then choose a card from the pile with your right hand. Before turning over the card to reveal a specific letter, meditate on a particular question, issue, or problem you're facing. Ask the Kabala for guidance in these matters, and then turn over the card. Find the corresponding essay for the letter you've chosen in the book, and read carefully.

The letters are meditation aids to help you focus with clarity on a particular situation and bring about the positive outcome you seek. Each letter brings to the table certain energies and a unique level of consciousness. When you're able to recognize those energies, you'll see what it is you're looking for in each page.

As you pose questions on a regular basis, you'll find that the Kabala is in fact helping you refine your own intuitive capacities. Intuition is a form of intelligence that's context-bound, holistic and nurturing. It doesn't have a win/lose orientation; instead, it eavesdrops on the conversations of the universe.

In time, you'll come to know intuitively what each letter symbolizes for you and will be able to meditate on that letter independently, without having to reread the corresponding text. And with practice, you'll become increasingly aligned with the energies of the universe. *Ask the Kabala* will help you get there.

CHAPTER ONE

A Brief History of Kabala

*T*wo of the oldest Indian meditations are centered on the sounds "ahhh" and "ohhhm." The "ahhh" meditation is done in the morning, and is meant to bring about the things you want to manifest in the physical world. The "ohhhm" is said in the evening, to balance the energies within you and between you and the universe. When you put these two sounds together, interestingly, you have the same sound pattern found in the Hebrew word shalom (shahhhlohhhm"), which means "peace," "hello," "good-bye," and so much more. This is a perfect example of the mysteries that lie behind even the simplest things, such as words and letters.

What Is Kabala?

The Hebrew word *kabala* comes from the root *kabel,* meaning "to receive." Kabala is a body of mystical writings based on a book called the Zohar (also known as "The Book of Enlightenment"), which is an interpretation of the books known together as the Oral Torah.

The Written Torah, also called the Five Books of Moses, the Old Testament, or simply Torah, is the original text of the Jewish faith. The Oral Torah interprets the Torah and applies it to daily life, while the Zohar focuses on why a person should choose to live his or her life in this way. And the "why," it turns out, is incredibly simple: because living your life as a fully awakened and spiritual being is the most powerful thing you can ever achieve. It is also the most difficult thing to do, because it entails letting go of your outer constructs and focusing on the internal aspects of yourself.

Kabala strives to bring us to a pre-biblical consciousness, a realm of timeless values that existed prior to organized religion. This state of being is one of simple Godliness: It is the moment before you say a prayer, when you close your eyes and just feel the power of forces beyond comprehension, rather than the words of the prayer or the way in which they're said.

To function on a mystical, kabalistic level, you have to be willing to let things in and to accept forces beyond and above your control. To receive, in this case, is also to let go: to let go of your preconceived notions, your ego and your fear. By allowing ourselves to receive and embrace the knowledge and the awareness of kabalistic thinking, we will soon be able to tap into the energy that connects all things and brings greater meaning to our lives.

Where Does the Kabala Come From?

Long before the Torah was written, Abraham, the first Jew, is said to have written a book called *Sefer Yetzira* (or the "Book of Creation"), the first book written in Hebrew, and the first to describe the energies of the planets and the zodiac. This work can also be read as a meditative guide to channeling the energies of the universe for a variety of different purposes.

Throughout time, there were always groups of students who were tuned in to the deeper levels of meaning in the Torah, and who studied the *Sefer Yetzira* with all of its mystical teachings. Eventually, these clusters of sages came to be known as Kabalists.

One student in particular, Rabbi Shimon bar Yochai, hid in a cave with his son Rabbi Eliezer for 13 years, writing down the lessons of the mystical world. The result of these years was the *Sefer HaZohar,* a mystical interpretation of the Torah written in ancient Aramaic—today, it's simply known as the Zohar.

In the Zohar, Rabbi Shimon bar Yochai lays out the basic concept of the ten *Sefirot* (dimensions or energy levels) used by God to create the universe. Each *sefirah,* or sphere, represents certain aspects of humanity and its quest to seek out meaning through understanding God and the universe. They're often presented in a chart formed in the shape of a person, each *sefirah* corresponding to a part of the body and the human psyche.

To give you an overview of this very elaborate system, the top three levels (*Keter:* Crown; *Hochma:* Wisdom; and *Bina:* Understanding) are considered to be beyond human understanding; the middle six (*Hesed:* Love; *Gevurah:* Strength; *Tiferet:* Beauty; *Netzach:*

Eternity; *Hod:* Splendor; and *Yesod:* Foundation) correspond to the increasingly complex ways in which a person can access God; and the last level (*Malchut:* Kingship) represents the physical world.

Each *sefirah* has its own characteristics and energy intelligence, and has a whole host of meanings, corresponding symbols, and so forth. This is only the beginning of an increasingly rich and complex system of associations that takes you deeper and deeper into an understanding of the universe.

Uncovering the Hidden Tradition

For generations, Kabala was held back from the general public. There were dozens of reasons why people were discouraged from studying the Zohar: for example, it was said that these works were so powerful that they should only be read by married men over the age of 40 because they'd gained the necessary knowledge and maturity. In other words, the mystical powers contained in the Zohar were thought to be too overwhelming to be used by the general populace. Scholars who understood the power of these texts feared what might happen should they fall into the hands of evildoers.

More likely, these restrictions and warnings were simply meant to cover up the fact that the Zohar was an incredibly complex text written in ancient Aramaic, which few people could decode well enough to teach. By the time it was translated—and communications had reached a stage advanced enough that scholars were able to interpret the text into comprehensible explanations, making the book accessible to the public—many generations had elapsed. Today we have access to the texts, as well as to dozens of books that help us understand them and apply them to our lives.

Within the Zohar, there's a prediction that in the Age of Aquarius, everyone will know about the secrets of the Kabala because they'll be essential principles of life. Scientific knowledge and advancement was necessary in order to bring about the Age of Aquarius, where all people recognize the laws of nature. That time is now. Our amazing access to information, through resources like the Internet and our generally global world, make this the time when accessing this long-hidden information is possible.

It took the catastrophic events of the last century—including the Holocaust, terrible wars, and most recently, September 11—for people to want to explore the deeper ends of their spiritual traditions, to find solace for the confusing and cruel world. Now that we're here, we have an opportunity to learn about the principles of the Kabala, and to access a world that's been hidden from us for so long.

CHAPTER TWO

The Mysteries of the Aleph-Bet

The Zohar teaches that the Torah is made of black fire on white fire. That is to say that the black fire represents the actual letters written on the physical Torah scroll, while the white fire is the space in between and surrounding each letter. Together, these two elements make up the whole picture we know as the Torah; and the white, blank space is just as crucial as the black markings that make up the letters and words we read. Black fire, the Kabala says, is the simple, literal meaning of the text, the part we can understand intellectually, whereas the white fire is the more contemplative side, the part we must find for ourselves by interpreting, assessing, and emotionally connecting to the material.

Some rabbis write that the black-fire Torah

is the one we have in this world, but in the world to come, when we have reached a higher spiritual plain, we will be able to read the Torah of white fire. In other words, the parts of life that are hidden from us, the things we do not see immediately with our five senses, are just as important for us as anything else, perhaps even more important. But until we reach the level of being able to "see" the white fire, we first need to focus on what we can learn from the black.

Numbers and Letters

The Kabala teaches us that it is possible to interpret and reinterpret the traditional stories and fables of the Torah into infinite levels of meaning. By using meditation techniques, we can come to see deeper into stories than we ever imagined possible. By looking at the Hebrew letters that form the words in the books of Torah, we can see shapes and figures that illustrate the stories their words describe. And by using *gematria* (an ancient form of sacred mathematics in which every letter is given a numerical value and then analyzed according to the numbers that each word adds up to), we can bring ourselves to a state of mind where even the letters themselves have many levels of meaning. This then changes our perception of words, and adds to the multiple interpretations of the Torah.

As kabalists have said for thousands of years, we humans are a microcosm of the universe. This is a reference to the fact that there are 22 letters in the Hebrew language, and 22 chromosomes in the human body—there's even a myth that God actually created the human being using the letters of the alphabet. Aside from that theory, we can also draw the conclusion that we as people are intensely linked to the letters that form our history, and find ways of seeing ourselves in their very makeup.

In short, kabalists teach that there are infinite ways to manipulate words and letters, and hundreds of techniques that turn sentences upside down and backward until they speak to us from every angle imaginable. Just as the equation $E=mc^2$ is so much more than a conglomeration of letters and numbers (it's the symbolic abbreviation for an incredibly complex law of nature), every letter in the *Aleph-Bet* stands for so much more than itself.

One interesting example of *gematria* is the word *Kabala* itself. Using the numerical value assigned to the letters on page 16, we can see that the letters that comprise this word are: *Kuf* (100), *Bet* (2), *Lamed* (30), and *Heh* (5), together totaling 137. In quantum physics, the most important—and most basic—code number is the "pure number," which describes the exact energy at which the entire universe vibrates. This number is represented as alpha, which is defined by the speed of light, and has a value of 1/137, the reciprocal value of the word *Kabala*.

When you start to dig a little deeper, you'll discover that there are endless numbers of words whose numerical value add up to something much more. In addition to *gematria*, kabalists also use the theory of *a't'ba'sh*, in which every letter corresponds to the letter at the very opposite end of the alphabet, so that *Aleph*, the first letter, equals *Tav*, the last, and *Bet*, the second letter, equals *Shin*, the second-to-last letter, and so on. With just these two formulas in mind, you can begin to imagine the levels of meaning that it's possible to create.

The Hebrew Letters: An Overview

Before you become too overwhelmed by how to invert, count, and rearrange the letters of the *Aleph-Bet* into infinite interpretations, let's look at the letters themselves.

It's important to see the characters and how they're drawn. You'll notice that some letters are very similar, while others are clearly composites of one another. The physical appearance of each of the letters is just as significant as the numerical or inverted value. The *Vav*, for instance, is often spoken about in Kabala as the straight line of Divine light that descended from the heavens to the earth at the first moment of creation; therefore, it's drawn as a straight, vertical line. The *Shin* is made up of three *Vavs* and a connecting line at the bottom, symbolizing the connections and similarities between different worlds.

Take a look:

LETTER	HEBREW SYMBOL	NUMERICAL VALUE
Aleph	א	1
Bet	ב	2
Gimmel	ג	3
Dalet	ד	4
Heh	ה	5
Vav	ו	6
Zayin	ז	7
Chet	ח	8
Tet	ט	9
Yud	י	10
Caph	כ	20
Lamed	ל	30
Mem	מ	40
Nun	נ	50
Samech	ס	60
Ayin	ע	70
Peh	פ	80
Tzaddik	צ	90
Kuf	ק	100
Resh	ר	200
Shin	ש	300
Tav	ת	400

If the Hebrew letters are new to your eye, take some time to let their shapes sink in. You may find yourself gravitating toward groups of letters, or one in particular—perhaps the first letter of your name is the one you'll want to explore initially. Since every letter of every word brings with it a distinct energy, it's important to be familiar with these building blocks of the Hebrew language.

The Physical Torah

As with everything in the world, there's nothing accidental about the way a Torah scroll is produced. First of all, to be a fully "kosher" Torah that can be used in a synagogue service, the scroll must be made of parchment, and every letter must be handwritten by a scribe, called a *Sofer*, who's specially trained in the art of biblical calligraphy. Not only must every letter be perfectly drawn by hand, but if ever a letter or even part of a letter becomes scratched or smudged, it must be repaired in order to be used again.

This may seem overzealous to our modern sensibilities—after all, can't we just read from the professionally printed books with the same text written in it? Why should it matter if the corner of one letter is slightly smudged? The answer is that for centuries kabalists have said that every human soul is compared to a single letter in the Torah scroll. Consequently, if just one person is damaged—that is, if one member of the group is somehow impaired or hidden—then we must first work toward repairing him or her before we can continue as a whole. Just as your life would be unfulfilling if you focused only on yourself, the Torah cannot function without its readers.

Another amazing thing about the way the Torah scroll is written is that it must be done with the completely pure intention of the scribe. This painstaking and difficult process can take an incredible amount of time to complete, and requires serious training and concentration. In addition to the pressure of producing something that is, in essence, completely perfect, the scribe must also have pure thoughts when writing the scroll, constantly thinking of the good of the community who will read from his or her work. As with all things, the motivation of the scribe has to be one of sharing and positive energy.

Stories and Their Kabalistic Significance

The Torah scroll contains the Five Books of Moses, or the Old Testament. Written by hand on parchment through the generations, this book contains all the major myths and archetypal stories that form the foundation of the Jewish faith.

The Torah, kabalists say, is like a blueprint for life: Everything that's included in the handwritten scroll has something to teach us about our own lives even to this day. While you may not be able to relate to Moses parting the Red Sea or a description of the Holy Temple service today, you *can* relate to modern miracles such as space travel and elaborate systems of prayer and devotion.

It's interesting to note that the very first word of the Torah, in Hebrew, starts not with an *Aleph,* which is the first letter of the alphabet, but with a *Bet,* the second letter: *"Bereishit bara Elohim* (In the beginning, God created . . .)." This is to teach us an essential lesson: Life is never as simple as it appears, and we can only see a tiny part of what's actually going on around us. We don't start with *Aleph* but with *Bet,* we start "in" the beginning (the letter *Bet* is the Hebrew prefix used to denote "in"), inside something that already exists on some level, something that's beyond our human comprehension.

Starting the Torah with the second letter instead of the first is the catalyst for the very essence of active spiritual life in that it begs the question "Why?" from the beginning. We must always strive to look beyond the surface and never take anything for granted. We weren't put here on this planet to get easy answers, and must always try to dig deeper and deeper until we reach our personal truths, until we can reveal the white fire surrounding the black fire that we see.

Some biblical scholars ponder the fact that the first and last letters of the Torah, *Bet* and *Lamed,* when inverted, spell the word *Lev,* which means "heart." If you look back to our chart of the Hebrew symbols for these letters, you'll notice that the *Bet* is formed with three closed sides and one open side, and the *Lamed* is open at the bottom and then reaches high up. These two letters epitomize openness and growth, perhaps to teach us that when we read the words of the Torah and come to understand them through Kabala, we should do so with an open heart and with the desire to grow on every level.

PART II

The Letter Cards

1

א
Aleph

אברם
Avram
(Abraham)

And God said to Abram, "Go for yourself from your land, from your relatives, and from your father's house to the land that I will show you. And I will make of you a great nation; I will bless you, and make your name great, and you shall be a blessing."

Genesis 12:1-2

With these words begins the long journey of Abraham, the father of monotheism and the first Jew, through arduous deserts and foreign lands toward the discovery of a new faith and a new way of relating to God.

Much has been said about why Abraham, of all people, was chosen for this task. The answer lies here: Beyond everything he later experiences, Abraham is first and foremost willing to take on this initial adventure, to leave behind all that is familiar to him—his country, his family, and his home—and begin again.

You'll notice that in this passage, Abraham's name is spelled "Abram." That's because this story takes place before he's truly proven himself, when he's still in his original state of mind. Abram must go through a series of trials and tribulations before God endows him with the holy letter *Heh,* signifying his close connection to the Divine. Abram's wife, Sarai, will also be renamed along the way, becoming Sarah, the first of the four matriarchs.

The Hebrew term *Lech Lecha,* which are the opening words of the passage, literally means "you go." In this instance, however, it's used in the figurative sense—Abram is instructed not just to get up and go, but to "go for yourself" or "go toward yourself."

In other words, this passage reflects something much deeper than a physical movement into the unknown. The real journey is an inner one: Abram must leave behind his comfortable way of life, which is full of assumptions, and look deeper into his heart to discover what lies beneath. He must disrupt his routine in order to find something much greater—that is, the deeper truths of life.

In kabalistic terms, this is the real greatness of the patriarch. He is the first to illuminate the path of self-discovery and "find himself." It's an active journey, one filled with many life-threatening risks and tests along the way, but it's perhaps the most rewarding of all. It's the journey that results in a new name, and a whole new life.

The appearance of the *Aleph* card may be a sign that you're unsure as to where your life is headed and that you want to know which direction to take. The *Aleph*, the first letter of the alphabet, comes at the start of a new adventure or at the end of an old cycle.

Focus on the energy of Abraham in order to **begin again**, as if from scratch. Envision leaving everything behind and walking day by day into new spiritual and emotional territory. You know not what lies ahead, nor which direction is correct, but the journey is yours for the taking.

Know that changing your life, and the lives of generations to come, begins with the very first step you take with faith in yourself and inner resolve.

2

ב
Bet

מגדל בבל
Migdal Bavel
(Tower of Babel)

The whole earth was of one language and of common purpose. And it came to pass, when they migrated from the east they found a plain in the land of Shinar and settled there. They said to one another, "Come, let us make bricks and burn them in fire." And the brick served them as stone, and the lime served them as mortar. And they said, "Come, let us build a city, and a tower with its top in the heavens, and let us make a name for ourselves, lest we be dispersed across the whole earth."

Genesis 11:1-9

As children, we're taught that the "Tower of Babel" story is a fable used to explain why we humans speak so many different languages and why we live in so many different corners of the world. We're not often told the more sophisticated truth, which is that after the people built their famous tower (imagining that they could reach the heavens and from there rage against God), they were punished with the very thing they sought to avoid: dispersion throughout the world, as well as different languages.

This dispersion is considered a punishment, for now the people who once were of "common purpose" are many different peoples, filled with differences and conflicts—a state of affairs that will lead to unrest beyond anything they'd imagined.

The people of this early generation (the one following the first destruction of the world through the great flood, which we read about in the story of Noah) sought to use their unity of purpose against God instead of finding ways to use that gift for the good. They didn't appreciate the gift of Oneness they'd been given, so they were punished with the very opposite state of affairs: They'd now face the challenge of having to learn to understand one another linguistically, culturally, and even geographically before they could accomplish anything as a group. They were reduced to a tower of babble—no one could understand a word anyone else said—and confusion (the Hebrew word *mebubal* means "confused").

Today, we know no other reality than one of diversity and cultural dissonance. But at the beginning of time, we were One. This Oneness, which is also a sign of closeness to God, was not able to withstand even a relatively short period of human history. The rest of time would be a gradual coming together again, a journey of *Tikkun Olam* (Healing the World) that would take thousands of years to achieve.

In our 21st-century world, we're just beginning to experience the spiritual repair, the *Tikkun,* for the Tower of Babel. Today we're a global society; we understand each other's languages; and we deal with one another on political, economic, and social levels all the time. The world is still in disrepair, but it's getting a little better every day.

The letter *Bet,* which corresponds to the number two, is also the first letter of the Torah. This is to teach us that nothing is ever as apparent as we'd like it to be. Starting the Torah with *Bet* instead of *Aleph* suggests that it's important to always look at two sides of every picture—and never take anything for granted. We must see things from both the spiritual and material angles, from the black and white perspectives, and from as many points of view as possible.

This is the lesson of Babel: To think that we as a human population can band together to change the forces of nature or to rebel against higher forces over which we have no control is the ultimate hubris. For this mistake, we needed to be separated and given different languages and spaces, to be spread about in such an extreme way that we long for the way things used to be, and to try to repair that damage so that we can one day become united for good.

The *Bet* card comes to you in times of **conflict**. You're seeing things in one way when you need to be looking at the situation from any number of alternate angles. Consider the question at hand from different perspectives, putting yourself in the opposite position and thinking about the various ways in which you can be proactive instead of merely reactive.

Meditate on the story of the Tower of Babel.

Imagine the heat of anger that prompted those people to build a mammoth tower.

Now breathe . . . and imagine how the world might have been had we not assumed that our strength and power could literally climb into the heavens and change the force of nature.

Nothing is as simple as we first assume; instead, life is a complicated web of perspectives and priorities. You can only find peace when you see things from many angles and then come to understand your own heart more truly.

3

ג

Gimmel

גר

Ger
(The Stranger)

When a stranger dwells among you in your land, do not taunt him. The stranger who dwells with you shall be like a native among you, and you shall love him like yourself, for you were strangers in the land of Egypt.

Leviticus 19:33-34

The Old Testament repeats the theme of "love thy neighbor" many times, reminding us of our own times as "strangers in a strange land" so that we'll be more sensitive to others in repressed or minority status. Because of your own history of enslavement, whether literal or figurative, you should know how it feels to be out of your element, and make an effort to include and accept those peoples who are different from you but who dwell in your midst.

Although the time the Jews spent in Egypt was one of oppression, slavery, and humiliation, there was also a sense of having settled there, for better or worse. In fact, when Moses led the Jews out of Egypt and began the journey toward the Promised Land and liberation, half of the former slaves chose to stay behind, because to them, a familiar reality, even a horrible one, seemed better than the unknown. Even those who left with Moses at one point panicked in the face of the difficult journey and wondered if maybe they would have been better off back in Egypt, where at least they knew their routines.

In a way, this desire to return to slavery makes sense—after so many years of living in one harsh reality, it's an enormous task to change one's mind-set to that of a free people. This is why we must be kind to the stranger, to encourage him to adapt to his new environment rather than returning to a damaging past. And even if the stranger is just "passing through" and not necessarily joining our specific community, we should encourage him to get the most out of his journey while he's on it.

The word *Ger* is usually translated as "convert," and the verb form, *Lagor*, means "to dwell." In this passage, we see that a *Ger* is not only someone who has officially converted into a new society or religion, but also a stranger, a foreigner who lives among a new set of people and customs. We've all been *Gers* at one point or another: We've moved to a new city, left home to go off to college, been transferred for work, traveled in faraway countries, or simply changed the way we look at the world, so we've all become converts of sorts along the way.

To some extent, this "strangeness," the definition of a "stranger in a strange land" is essential to Kabala. It may seem odd that this phrase is used in a positive way in traditional texts. But when you look at it from a kabalistic angle, it makes perfect sense: Sometimes you need to lose yourself in order to find yourself, sometimes you need chaos in order to show you the path to order and enlightenment, and sometimes you need to take the road less traveled in order to find the right path for you.

The *Gimmel* comes to you when you're suffering from improper **judgment.** You're either feeling judged or are judging others unfairly, whether you realize it or not. You may feel like an outsider at work, in social gatherings, or spiritually. Conversely, you may feel *too much* like an insider, so much so that you don't accept anyone outside of your immediate circle.

The challenge is one of identity: We all have to strike a fine balance between knowing who we are and where we've come from, and accepting the Other in our lives as equally valid. This is certainly not an easy task. Knowing oneself is hard enough; accepting the Other is sometimes nearly impossible.

Open yourself to new and different experiences: Hear the stories of the people you encounter on your life's journey and appreciate where they've been, and share your own stories of exile and redemption. Only by opening to others and accepting them will you enlarge your worldview and be totally at peace with your own life.

4

ד
Dalet

לדבק
LeDavek
(To Cleave)

And God said, "It is not good that man be alone; I will make him a helper corresponding to him"... So God cast a deep sleep upon the man and he slept; and he took one of his sides and He filled in flesh in its place. Then God fashioned the side that He had taken from the man into a woman, and He brought her to the man, and the man said, "This time it is bone of my bones and flesh of my flesh. This shall be called Woman, for from man was she taken." Therefore a man shall leave his father and his mother and cleave to his wife, and they shall become one flesh.

Genesis 2:18, 21-24

Adam, the first man, was given the task of naming all the plants and animals of the earth. In the process, he realized that every animal had a mating partner, yet he was alone in the world. None of the animals seemed to make a match for him, and none of them had the powers of reason or language with which he'd been blessed.

Eventually, Adam became saddened by this fact, so God created Woman. At first, Adam was so taken aback by this creature, a human being literally made from a part of him and obviously meant to be his partner in life, that he couldn't find the right name for her. Instead, he used the term *this* to describe his new helper!

The Woman represented a new reality for Adam. Although he possessed the ability to name the animals almost immediately and instinctively, when faced with another human being he became somewhat speechless. The Woman, in other words, presented the challenge for Adam of being faced with an equal partner.

In fact, the phrase *ezer kenegdo* (translated here as "a helper corresponding to him") literally means "a helper in opposition to him."

This isn't meant to be taken negatively; rather, when two people who are really meant to be together are united, they help each other by challenging one another—by rendering the other speechless in a way—so that they learn a new way of relating to the world, and thereby come into themselves as fully aware adults.

Soon, the Woman we later know as Eve (*Chava* in Hebrew) will eat from the forbidden fruit of the Tree of the Knowledge of Good and Evil, and the couple will be banished from the Garden of Eden as a result, setting in motion the long history of mankind—one that's filled with strife and pain as well as pleasure. But here, in these first moments of her creation, Adam realizes that their union is something that will never happen in the same way again. Men and women will mate, but they will never again be created from the same flesh and bones, and Adam recognizes this very clearly.

The Hebrew verb *LeDavek* means "to cleave," to hold onto something tightly. Just as two people literally become one in the sexual act, they also become one emotionally and spiritually when they unite as life partners and decide to create a new family unit together. To do this with a full heart, they have to leave behind their first home, their primary connections to their parents and siblings, and put this new person before all of them. This sort of tight bond needs to be taken very seriously and done with incredible intent—in other words, in order to form a real and lasting marriage, you have to cleave to one another unlike you have to anyone else before.

The letter *Dalet*, however, is not one of closing off but rather openness. Notice its shape: a vertical line and short horizontal line at the top. The character is shaped with two open sides, illustrating the sort of wide-open willingness you need to possess in order to find that partner to whom you'll want to cleave.

The first union is like the ultimate yin/yang dichotomy: Adam and Eve are made of the same materials, yet they're opposites. They complete one another and form a whole new unit from which the rest of the world will be born, yet they are, from the very beginning, extremely different people with different approaches to life. Although they didn't face the same challenges we do today (they only had one another to choose from, whereas we have thousands of potential mates from which to choose!), they're still our first model of being open enough to one person to close ourselves off from the rest.

※ ※

The *Dalet* card represents **paradox in relationship.** Just as Eve was both the ultimate partner for Adam and the cause of his lifetime of suffering, our spiritual endeavors are both what bring us closer to our ultimate fulfillment and what keeps us up at night wondering what the meaning of life is.

Deveikut, the act of cleaving, is not just used in terms of romantic relationships. Lovers cleave to one another, yes, but individuals also cleave to support networks, and souls cleave to a higher force that sustains them in darker times. And it's often the person or idea with which we have the most difficult time that teaches us the greatest of lessons.

Focus on the open side of the *Dalet* and allow yourself to be open to dependence. You'll always be your unique self, although you may often fear losing that self by being absorbed into another person's life. Just know that the relationships you enter, if you're open to them sufficiently, have the power to create whole new worlds.

5

ה
Heh

הנני
Hinenni
("Here I Am")

Moses was shepherding the sheep of Jethro, his father-in-law, the priest of Midian; he guided the sheep far into the wilderness, and he arrived at the Mountain of God, toward Horeb. An angel of God appeared to him in a blaze of fire amid the bush. He saw, and behold! The bush was burning in the fire but the bush was not consumed. Moses thought, "I will turn aside now and look at this great sight—why will the bush be not burned?" God saw that he had turned aside to see; and God called out to him from amid the bush and said, "Moses, Moses!" and he replied, "Here I am!"

Exodus 3:1-4

The episode of the burning bush signifies the beginning of the Exodus from Egypt simply because it is the event that makes Moses into a prophet, completing his personal transition. Moses went from being an orphaned infant (when his mother put him in a basket in the Nile river to save him from Pharaoh's evil decree against all male Hebrew babies), to a prince (having been adopted by the Pharaoh's daughter and raised in the palace), to a shepherd (when he becomes aware of his true identity and runs away from Egypt, joining Jethro in Midian and marrying his daughter), to finally becoming the great leader we know—the liberator—at this moment in the wilderness.

Just as he had to go through many transitions and changes in his life before he was ready to fulfill his destiny of freeing the Jewish people from slavery, Moses' prophecy itself has several stages: (1) He goes out into the wilderness; (2) he sees an angel; (3) he notices that the bush is on fire but is not consumed, and (4) only then does the voice of God make itself heard. And when God speaks to Moses, He has to say his name twice, so that Moses will be sure that what he's hearing is real, and not just a figment of his imagination.

After all of these stages of increasing awareness, Moses replies, simply, *"Hinneni"* ("Here I am"), the same word used by Abraham, Isaac, and Jacob in their times of prophecy.

The direct reply may seem startling—after all, God obviously knows that Moses is "there" or He would not have revealed Himself. But when you think about it, it makes perfect sense: Moses needed to make sure that this was real—he needed to look in the direction of the bush; clarify what was happening; hear his name being called; and affirm that, yes, he was ready to receive the message that would now be sent to him, and would accomplish the task that would soon be set out before him. His whole life has been a slow building-up to this point: where he could acknowledge his own powers and answer God directly, entering into a dialogue with Him that would not only change the course of history, but change the prophet's own life completely.

Bible commentators point out that the spot on which the burning bush appeared to Moses was actually the same spot on which the Torah would be given many years later—Mt. Sinai. The fact that Moses' first awakening to his role as a prophet and his most important task in that role happened on the same spot is not accidental. Just as Moses needed to acknowledge his place in this epic story, so will every single one of his followers need to acknowledge themselves at the giving of the Torah and the Revelation that comes along with it.

The letter *Heh* corresponds to the number five, which is also the number of physical senses we're given at birth: sight, hearing, touch, taste, and smell. But there's a sixth sense, too: the one we associate with spirituality, which can only be accomplished on our own, through our own journeys to new levels of awareness and emotional depth. This is the sixth sense that Moses acknowledges at the burning bush, and it is that sense that will help him through all the trials and tribulations of leading a people out of slavery and into freedom.

In order to reach that sixth sense, we learn from the word *Hinneni,* we must first master the original five senses, getting to know ourselves in our literal, physical states and eventually learning how to get beyond that limited world to the miraculous world that lies above and beyond.

The *Heh* card comes to you at moments of **transition** and significant personal growth. You may be moving from one phase of your life into another, reaching a certain landmark age or accomplishment, or simply be in the process of maturation and deepening. You've gone as far as you can go according to your limited physical understanding of one phase, and you're on the brink of developing your own sixth sense.

Take the time to understand where you've been and how your whole life has brought you to this point in time and place in the world. Nothing is accidental—after all, the same mountain on which Moses sees the burning bush is the same place where Abraham bound Isaac and where the Torah was given. So don't take even the slightest details for granted.

Know that by answering the call, by being present in the moment of transition and being able to say *"Hinneni,"* you're accomplishing more than you ever have before.

6

ו
Vav

וידוי
Vidui
(Confession)

When a man or woman who commits any of man's sins, by committing treachery toward God, and that person shall become guilty—they shall confess the sin that they committed; he shall make restitution for his guilt in its principle amount and add unto it a fifth, and give it to the one to whom he is indebted.

Numbers 5:6-7

The Jewish concept of confession and atonement for sins is based on this verse from the Bible, in which a person is dishonest regarding financial issues (theft, withholding salary, cheating a person on a loan, and so forth). Because these sins are considered not just an affront to the victim but also to God, God requires the sinner to repent, confess, and pay back the money he's stolen with interest before he can be forgiven.

The main prayer service of Yom Kippur, the Day of Atonement, is called the *Vidui,* which means "confession," not "atonement." It may seem odd that the main service of the heart on this holiest day of the year is filled with confessions that the penitent is meant to say aloud, sometimes together with the rest of congregation. After all, isn't repentance an inner process, a personal discussion one has with God? The answer is yes and no. Although we repent in our hearts, without confession—that is, the act of saying "I have sinned" and admitting our guilt—we'll never truly repent, gain atonement, or be able to move on, repairing the damage we have done.

The letter *Vav* is most commonly known as the prefix used to denote the word "and," and is seen hundreds of times thought the Bible as such, connecting words and concepts. *Vidui* serves a similar purpose: Because your past informs your present and future, being honest with yourself—that is, admitting your faults and expressing remorse for the things you've done wrong—will help to connect that past to the future in a more productive way. Expressing your guilt out loud and facing the consequences allows you to move on with your life and will help you truly reach a state of self-knowledge.

It's especially interesting to note that in Judaism the *Vidui* is said not only on Yom Kippur, but on one's wedding day and on one's deathbed. At traditional Jewish weddings, the bride and groom immerse in the *mikveh* (ritual bath), fast for the day leading up to their wedding, and recite Yom Kippur prayers just before they go to their ceremony. The bride also traditionally wears a white dress and the groom a white robe, called a *kittl*, which will in the future be worn to synagogue on Yom Kippur every year and eventually serve as his clothing for burial. The wedding day is known as a personal Yom Kippur for the couple, a day to reflect on their lives up until this point, realize what was lacking in those lives, and purify themselves both physically and spiritually for the future.

The connections—the *Vavs*—between these three moments in life (the Day of Atonement, marriage, and death) are more than symbolic. The *Vidui* brings us to a place of purification and self-awareness that is crucial in every major life-changing event. Recognizing your shortcomings once a year, working toward a clean slate with which to start your married life, and making peace with God before you die are all essential elements of a truly fulfilled existence.

The *Vav* card comes to you in times when it's important to make a confession of some kind. This need not be a "sin" and isn't a sign of any shortcomings. It's just that from time to time we all need to admit certain truths to ourselves, to face up to our actions out loud, and **accept responsibility** for what we've done.

The past will haunt you until it's been properly dealt with, so don't wait to take control of your life. Allow yourself to say what needs to be said. The rest will follow.

7

ז
Zayin

זכור את יום השבת
Zachor et Yom HaShabbat
(Remember the Sabbath Day)

Remember the Sabbath day to sanctify it. Six days shall you work and accomplish all your work, but the seventh day is a Sabbath to the Lord, your God; you shall not do any work—you, your son, your daughter, your slave, your maidservant, your animal, and your stranger who dwells within your gates—for in six days God made the heavens and the earth, the sea and all that is in them, and He rested on the seventh day. Therefore, God blessed the Sabbath day and sanctified it.

Exodus 20:8-11

Zayin is the seventh letter of the alphabet, so it makes sense that the commandment to observe the day of rest, the Sabbath (which is the seventh day of the week in Judaism) begins with the word *Zachor* ("remember"). Why is the commandment to "remember" and "sanctify" rather than to "do" something active? And why does the passage say that not only should the heads of household cease from working, but the whole extended family should, too—down to the animals?

Abraham Joshua Heschel, one of the great Jewish philosophers of the 20th century, wrote that the Sabbath brings us into the realm of time and away from that of space. Because we spend our whole lives envisioning the world in terms of physical things—objects we want to own, places we want to see, and so on—it's important to take a day to focus on the invisible objects like "sacred moments" in time. You can't see, touch, or hear a spiritual experience, but you feel it on a higher level, and you may remember it every day for the rest of your life.

If you were to climb to the top of a mountain and take in the view, the sensation you'd feel—that awareness of the beauty of nature—is an experience of time, not space.

You appreciate the physical view, yes, but your feeling of being at one with that physical world is entirely spiritual. This is what happens on the seventh day of creation: God has created the heavens and the earth, the seas, the animals and plants and humankind; and finally, on the seventh day, He takes a look at everything He's done, decides to take a break, and makes that break a regular part of the rhythm of life on earth—a holy part.

The Sabbath is the first thing in all of creation that's described as "holy." But how can you sanctify something that isn't physical? How can a day, which is nothing more than a mental concept we use to mark time and keep track of history, become a holy object? Heschel answered that celebrating the Sabbath is a way of celebrating the "holiness of time," a way to take control of our lives and focus on ourselves. And to do this properly, we not only have to cease from physical labor, but we need to place ourselves in an environment where everything around us, and everyone in our lives, also makes this break.

For six days of the week we use our powers to dominate the world around us—working, building, creating new objects, and the like.

It's important, then, to use the seventh day to build up *ourselves,* to cease working and just appreciate the beauty of the world around us. It's as if the entire week is the hike to the top of the mountain, and the Sabbath is the rest we take when we get to the top—where we can finally see everything from a new perspective.

In every religion there is a Sabbath day, though which day of the week it is varies from tradition to tradition. What unites them all is the concept of a day sanctified and set apart from the rest of the week. The concept of a day of rest is integral to Kabala as well—it's the very heart of the act of restriction, the structure in our lives that allows us to gain so much by simply doing less.

The *Zayin* card is a reminder that you need to stop and allow yourself to experience **stillness.**

Weeks go by in endless repeating cycles of actions and experiences—work, eat, sleep; work, eat, sleep. We often think of periods of rest as a waste of time, but the truth is that stillness, meditation, and experiences of spirituality are the most rewarding moments of our life.

Knowing and appreciating the value of the Sabbath day is one thing—remembering it, *Zachor,* is something different altogether. Knowing is theoretical; remembering is practical.

Find a way to make the Sabbath a reality for you, a holy time apart from the rest of your week where you can just *be* and need not *do* anything.

8

ח
Chet

חלה
Challah

...when you will eat of the bread of the Land, you shall set aside a portion for God. As the first of your kneading you shall set aside a loaf [Challah] as a portion, like the portion of the threshing-floor, so shall you set it aside.

Numbers 15:19-20

The Bible mentions the concept of "setting aside" many times: Corners of the field are to be set aside for the poor; the first fruits of every season are to be brought as offerings during harvest festivals; animals are brought as sacrifices in the Temple period; and ten percent of one's earnings is to be set aside for charity. In this case, Jews are instructed to set aside a portion of the first loaf of every batch of bread they bake for the High Priest.

Today, when there's no longer a Holy Temple at the center of Jewish ritual life, and Priests don't serve the same function, the commandment shifts: A piece of dough is taken from the first batch and thrown into the back of the oven to burn, symbolizing the destruction of the Temple and the exile that exists because of that destruction. There are many customs to reflect the loss of the Temple, such as replacing sacrifices with prayer services, using salt on bread to symbolize the bitterness of living in an imperfect world, and leaving a small part of a newly built home unfinished to commemorate the physical destruction of the Temple structure.

But "Taking *Challah*," as the custom is called, is more than merely preserving an ancient and now practically irrelevant commandment. By physically removing a small piece of dough and making it inedible, eventually discarding it altogether, we remind ourselves that everything we own is temporary. You may think that all of the dough is yours—after all, you paid for the ingredients, mixed them together, and watched them rise—but really, nothing belongs to you alone. You're given the wheat and the eggs and the water from a higher source, and by letting some of it go, you're acknowledging that source.

The root of *Challah* actually has nothing to do with bread (which is called, in Hebrew, *lechem*). Instead, the root is *chol,* which means "ordinary." The days of the week are separated into *Shabbat* and *chol,* Sabbath and weekday. *Challah,* a food made holy despite its ordinary origins, is made especially to be eaten on the Sabbath. Something as plain as wheat is elevated to a level at which it can be blessed and sanctified as an integral part of the Sabbath meal.

The concept of *Challah* extends into our daily lives: We all need to learn the kabalistic lesson of sharing in order to balance the energy of the universe. What we own is never entirely ours, and we could never truly need every single object in our possession. It's crucial to make giving a part of our consciousness, whether it is to acknowledge the higher force that guards us all, to remember the harsher realities of life, or to give thanks for what we already have.

The *Chet* card comes to teach us how we can **let go** of what we do not need. We can survive on bread and water alone, yet we rely on incredible luxuries as if they were necessary.

It's time to let go. Donate clothes you no longer wear to a homeless shelter; take food supplies to a soup kitchen; make a list of your dependencies, and then set the list aflame. You will feel an increased freedom as a result.

9

ט
Tet

טוב
Tov
(Goodness)

And God saw all that He had made, and behold it was very good. And there was evening and there was morning the sixth day.

Genesis 1:31

At the end of the initial days of the creation, God looks at what He made and "saw that it was good" every time. But on the last day, after He has created humankind, and the world is in its final form, ready to function on its own, He declares it "very good." Many commentators point to the fact that although the world would still be a "good" place without human beings, with them, the world can fulfill its ultimate potential. Once humankind was created, the world became a "very good" place, in which anything could happen.

We don't often appreciate the world we live in and the mundane realities of our lives. Air to breathe, food to eat, soil to walk on, and sunlight to give us energy are all taken for granted. More important, not only do we take for granted the natural world around us and the daily miracles of life on Earth, but we get so caught up in our warped perception of things that the planet can often seem like a place filled with negative energy.

Take one look at a baby, and you'll remember what an amazing place our world is. The infant sees everything as new and wonderful, filled with bursting colors, sounds, and smells—it notices things we can barely perceive. This is the way the world must have looked to God on the sixth day of creation. By affirming its essential goodness, He encourages us to see the world afresh every day, rather than to take it for granted.

The *Tet* is the ninth letter of the alphabet, and its character is drawn as a nearly closed structure with a protected inner part. This represents the nine months of pregnancy, the state of being expectant and filled with excitement, wonder, and awareness about the miraculous happenings of nature. It also symbolizes actualization, the coming to fruition of the process of conception: birth, a new life, and the creation of a whole new world, a personal universe.

Tov, goodness, is our natural state of being. As infants we're inherently good, linked only to nature. It's only when we grow up and distance ourselves from our inborn goodness that we forget to appreciate the little miracles of everyday life.

This declaration from the beginning of time teaches us to be thankful for the world we live in right now, rather than waiting until we're old and fragile and looking back on our lives. We should strive to look at the world as if it's being created anew every day.

The *Tet* card brings you to a state of **appreciation** for what you have in this world.

Do you only see what you don't have, such as the things you want to possess and the status you want to achieve? Or do you know that your life and your surrounding are *tov me'od*, very good?

Creation is not something that happened just once, at the beginning of time. Every breath is a new creation, every second is the start of a new existence. Losing sight of that is losing out on the good in our lives. So this card asks that you see the world through the eyes of a baby, and appreciate goodness.

10

י

Yud

יוסף
Yosef
(Joseph)

Then Joseph said to his brothers, "Come close to me, if you please," and they came close. And he said, "I am Joseph your brother—it is me, whom you sold into Egypt. And now, be not distressed, nor reproach yourselves for having sold me here, for it was to be a provider that God sent me ahead of you. For this has been two of the hunger years in the midst of the land, and there are yet five years in which there shall be neither plowing nor harvest. Thus God has sent me ahead of you to ensure your survival in the land and to sustain you for a momentous deliverance."

Genesis 45: 4-8

The story of Joseph is one of the most dramatic in all of history. Born to Jacob as the first child of his beloved wife, Rachel, Joseph is one of the 12 sons who will comprise the 12 tribes of Israel. But Joseph is unlike his brothers who are the sons of Leah and two maidservants—he's clearly the favorite and the spiritual inheritor of the family. He and his younger brother, Benjamin, who was born to Rachel just before her death, have always been treated differently than the other ten boys.

When, as a teenager, Joseph begins to have dreams of superiority—dreams in which he foresees that his brothers will one day bow down to him—his siblings decide that they've had enough of this "dreamer." They throw him into a dark pit and sell him into slavery. Afterward, they take his special multicolored tunic and soak it in blood as "proof" that he's been killed. They then return to Jacob and report their brother's "death."

However, rather than fading into obscurity and a life of slavery, once in Egypt Joseph is able to use his talents to rise to the top, interpreting dreams and gaining a reputation that will lead him to the Pharoah's palace to interpret the ruler's inexplicable visions.

When Joseph is able to see the hidden message in the Pharaoh's dreams of seven skinny cows eating seven fat ones as the sign of seven years of plenty followed by seven years of famine, he's promoted to be the Pharaoh's second in command and makes his way into the Egyptian leadership at a crucial time in history.

When the famine begins, Jacob sends his remaining sons to Egypt to gather provisions—and they come into contact with the brother they'd betrayed so many years ago. Not recognizing Joseph as an adult, his brothers bow down to the man they see as an Egyptian leader.

After many months of testing the men and sending them back and forth from Egypt to Canaan, Joseph finally reveals himself as their long-lost brother and sends for his father. After all this time, his original dream has finally come true: He's established himself in such a position of power that his brothers bow down to him, and they fear his revenge. But rather than express his anger and pain, Joseph tells them that he's come to realize that everything leading up to this point— their jealousy and their plot against him, his time served as a slave, and so forth—was all meant to be, because as a result, he was able to provide food for the family in a time of overwhelming famine.

Most of us cannot imagine being as "big" as Joseph was under the circumstances. Our anger over past wrongs becomes the dominant force in our actions. But Joseph, perhaps because of the amount of time that had passed, or because of his innate sense of the predestined nature of the world, looks at his reunion differently: He does want to make sure his brothers are sorry for their actions, but once he senses their remorse he seems to let go of his own anger and need for revenge. In this way, Joseph is able to focus on the present instead of the past, willing to move forward with his now reunited family.

Joseph's whole life has been one of dreams and their fulfillment. Having been born a dreamer, he's known all along that the images he saw in his mind weren't just figments of his imagination but signs of things that would actually come about in real life. As a young man, this awareness was looked at as snobbery, but as a mature adult, sobered by his difficult experiences, his gift was appreciated and led to the ultimate reunion of his family.

The *Yud*, as the smallest letter in the alphabet, is often thought about as a "point." This tiny point lies at the center of our hearts—it's the driving force that takes us from one stage of life to another, the motivation that follows us through every action we perform. Joseph suffered for his essential point (his talent), but with time it became clear to everyone that he was not just a dreamer but a prophet, and that all of his dreams would one day become reality.

The *Yud* appears in moments of spiritual or physical darkness. Like Joseph, you've been cast into a metaphorical pit and must redefine your life. You may feel misunderstood, underappreciated, or simply confused—the only way out of this darkness is by recognizing the small point in your soul that leads you forward in life.

Joseph teaches the power of believing in yourself. You must always know that your life is full of purpose, and that everything that happens to you occurs for a reason. The key to personal fulfillment lies in recognizing your uniqueness and then learning how to apply your special talents in order to change your world and come to an enlightened understanding of your past, present, and future.

Meditate on the power of **forgiveness.** Strive to be more like Joseph, who, as a result of forgiving his brothers for their actions, pulls his family together again.

11

כ
Caph

כָּלֵב
Calev (Caleb)

"But My servant Caleb, because a different spirit was with him and he followed Me wholeheartedly, I shall bring him to the Land to which he came, and his offspring shall possess it."

Numbers 14:24

After the great Exodus from Egypt, Moses led the Hebrew people to the Promised Land. But as they neared the border, the people became frightened and anxious. To ease their fears, Moses sent a delegation of spies, one from each tribe, to scout out the land and bring back a report to reassure the former slaves. The spies spent 40 days in the Land and came back with a difficult report: It was indeed full of milk and honey, but it was also filled with enemies of gigantic proportions—"We were like grasshoppers in our eyes, and so we were in their eyes!" they say (Num. 13:33).

When the people hear this report so soon after leaving Egypt, they're devastated. They can't understand why they must suffer so much, and wonder if they should go back to Egypt rather than face a future of war with an insurmountable enemy. But two of the spies, Joshua and Caleb, have a different perspective.

Caleb assures the people that they can conquer the enemies and the land; in fact, he tells them that the land is "very, very good," and that because they have God on their side, they have nothing to worry about. But the people don't listen to him.

When God hears of this event, He is enraged. After everything He's done to free the people from slavery and bring them to their own land, they still have little faith in their ability to move forward. So He decrees that except for Caleb and Joshua, who have seen things as they really are, no one from the original generation that escaped from

Egypt will be allowed to enter the Promised Land. Instead, this will be the beginning of 40 years of wandering in the desert, one year for every day the spies spent in the Land, and only when those 40 years pass and the first generation dies out will the younger generation be allowed to enter it.

What makes Caleb say "We can surely do it!" (Num. 13:30) when everyone else is clearly giving up hope? What distinguishes him and Joshua from the other spies and the rest of the people?

The spies say that "we were like grasshoppers in *our* eyes" when they describe the giants living in the land and the way they looked in comparison. That is to say, they *perceived themselves* as grasshoppers, insignificant and weak when compared to the inhabitants of the land. But that doesn't mean that they were so much smaller—it means that they'd lost their confidence, that they imagined themselves to be inferior, and that they saw the challenges ahead as impossible to overcome.

This happened because for years and years these people had suffered as slaves in Egypt, and they still felt like slaves: weak, small, and frightened by the big, strong taskmaster. The spies were, in a way, projecting their slave mentality onto the report they gave, and because the people were immersed in the same mentality, they believed it.

Caleb, on the other hand, had already gone beyond this mentality and was ready to accept the new realities of freedom and independence. Unfortunately, it would take 40 years of emotional work and psychological healing for the rest of the people to catch up with him.

Caph is considered to be a letter of **actualization**. Like the crown *(keter)* that symbolizes ultimate human power *(koach)*, the *Caph* represents an understanding of human potential and the realization of that potential.

Caph is also the first letter of the word *kavana*, an important term in Kabala. *Kavana* means "intention," or the energy with which you try to accomplish things. The outcome of your efforts is entirely bound up with your intention. Caleb had good intentions, and he tried to make others see what he saw. For that pure intent, he was rewarded with being able to enter into the Promised Land while everyone else was not.

Just as Caleb was able to see a different reality, and express his confidence in that reality, this card points to the fact that you should strive to look at things from a wider perspective, and not be hampered by your past.

12

ל
Lamed

לאה
Leah

Laban had two daughters. The name of the older one was Leah and the name of the younger one was Rachel. Leah's eyes were tender, while Rachel was beautiful of form and beautiful of appearance...

Genesis 29:16-17

When Jacob first saw Rachel, the daughter of his uncle Laban, he instantly fell in love with her. So much so, in fact, that he agreed to work for Laban for seven years in order to marry her. As the story goes, Jacob was so taken with Rachel that those years went by as if they were minutes.

But on their wedding night, Leah, the

older daughter, is sent to the wedding canopy in Rachel's place. In the morning, Jacob realizes that he's wed the wrong sister and confronts Laban. But what was done was done, so Jacob agrees to work another seven years in order to marry his true love. For the rest of their lives, the two sisters vie for Jacob's attention, raising a family that reflects their rivalry, despite the ultimate good that comes of it.

Deception is a big factor in this story: Not only does Laban trick Jacob, but Rachel also tricks him by giving her sister the secret signals that she and Jacob had made up in advance of the wedding so Leah wouldn't be embarrassed. And Leah also agrees to go through with the deception.

Commentators say that when Jacob woke up in the morning, he first confronted Leah, asking how she could have lied and pretended to be her sister. Leah responded that she'd acted much like her new husband, who once lied to his own father and pretended to be his evil twin brother, Esau, in order to get the blessing of the firstborn. With that reality as the basis for their marriage, it's no wonder that this love triangle is one of the most famous in history!

Leah is described as having had "tender" eyes—in other words, she's the less attractive of the sisters. While some biblical scholars say this description indicates that she was cross-eyed, others note that her eyes were damaged from excessive weeping, to the point where her vision was impaired.

Why was Leah crying so much, even before she met and married Jacob and entered her less-than-perfect relationship? According to kabalistic sources, Leah was predestined to marry Esau, and Rachel to marry Jacob; the two couples were then meant to produce 12 sons, each of whom would become the head of a tribe that would together comprise the Jewish nation. Leah, who knew that Esau was a man of the field who wouldn't follow his destiny, cried constantly over the fact that she wouldn't be able to fulfill her part in the history of her people as a result.

When Jacob meets Rachel, he's instantly smitten, not only because she's so beautiful, but because their match was "meant to be." When he marries Leah, he must work very hard to come to terms with the lies he's told in his life and the way they've all reconfigured the neat, orderly family saga as it was intended.

Leah is the one who best understands this situation, and although she'll suffer as the wife who's known to all as "second choice," she's comforted by being able to fulfill her destiny after all. By marrying Jacob and having six sons with him, she manages to become a matriarch after all.

Leah is the consummate example of a woman of valor—someone who suffers for her ideals, yet is unwavering in her faith and devotion. Throughout her long life with Jacob, the two develop a bond that in the end is stronger and more enduring than the bond that exists between him and Rachel. Because they had to conquer their anger at one another, and because her love for him was unreturned for so long (despite the family they were building together), Leah and Jacob represent a mature, adult relationship that deepens and blossoms with time. In the end, it is Leah who is buried next to Jacob when she dies, and it is Leah's children who will fulfill the more substantial roles in history as the heads of the Messianic line and the Priestly class.

The *Lamed* is the tallest letter of the alephbet, stretching far into the upper realms. It is the letter that spells the word *"lamed,"* meaning "learn" or "teach." Therefore, the *Lamed* represents a higher, spiritual form of knowledge.

The Kabala says that Leah represents the upper world of the *Shechina* (God's feminine form) revealed, whereas Rachel represents the lower world of the *Shechina* in exile. With this in mind, we can see another interpretation of Leah's "tender eyes": If eyes are the window into the soul, then Leah's soul is one that recognizes her own suffering. She's seen her path in life and taken control of it, changing the circumstances of her life in order to put things into place. Leah is clearly in charge of her own destiny—she's the one who reveals it.

The *Lamed* card comes to reflect the **inner knowledge** of Leah. Accept yourself and realize that any shortcomings you may think you have are, in essence, your strongest attributes. When you come to truly understand

and accept your destiny, you'll find ways to make it happen.

Reach up and look deep into the windows of your own soul—there you'll find the tools you need to make your dreams a reality.

13

מ
Mem

מרים
Miriam

When the Pharaoh's cavalry came with his chariots and horsemen into the sea and God turned back the waters of the sea upon them, the Children of Israel walked on the dry land amid the sea. Miriam the prophetess, the sister of Aaron, took her drum in her hand, and all the women went forth with drums and with dances. Miriam spoke up to them, "Sing to God, for He is exalted above the arrogant, having hurled horse with its rider into the sea."

Exodus 15:19-21

Miriam is one of the first female leaders in history, and specifically one of the first leaders of women. The scene described above takes place as the Jews are running out of Egypt to escape slavery, with Moses as their leader. When they come to the banks of the water and see the Pharaoh's army gaining on them in the distance, Moses performs the miracle of splitting the sea, and they're able to run on dry land. But when the last of the Jews has reached safety, the seas close back up, drowning the Pharaoh and all of his men and horses. When the people see this miraculous sight and realize that they've been saved yet again, they break out in song, and Miriam leads the women in their own unique celebration.

Miriam is called the "brother of Aaron" here to emphasize that even before their youngest brother, Moses, the epitome of prophecy, was born, Miriam herself had prophetic ability. In fact, some commentators say that it was Miriam who was responsible for Moses' birth in the first place. We know that she was the one to watch over his wicker basket on the banks of the Nile when the Pharaoh's daughter found him there, thus ensuring his safety—but did you know that without her there would have been no baby at all?

Miriam was six years old when her parents separated. The Pharaoh had decreed that all male babies born into Hebrew families would be thrown into the river to drown, whereas female babies could live. This was to ensure that the Pharaoh would remain a stronger dictator with less opposition.

Jochebed and Amram (along with many other couples) separated rather than take the risk of creating a child who would be condemned to a cruel death. Yet Miriam convinced her parents to remarry, arguing that the Pharaoh may have decreed against the boys, but by giving in to fear, Jochebed and Amram were in fact preventing even girls from being born. Furthermore, she'd seen into the future, and she knew before he was even conceived that Moses would be the savior of their people.

So it's because of his big sister that Moses was born, that he didn't drown in the river, and that he was adopted into the house of the Pharaoh, where he gained the leadership skills he'd need to become the leader of the Exodus.

Because of her unique gift of intuition from such an early age, Miriam was well loved among her people. And because she advocated that females take control of the situation, encouraging young wives to defy the Pharaoh's decree and continue to build their families, she's associated with the women's movement in its earliest stages. Feminists today place a Cup for Miriam alongside Elijah's at the Passover Seder table, symbolizing the many different kinds of salvation that exist for many different kinds of people.

The letter *Mem* is often associated with water *(mayyim),* and it's no coincidence that as they traveled in the desert, the Jewish people were accompanied by a miraculous wandering well of water given to them in the merit of Miriam's actions. When she died, the well dried up, signifying her crucial contribution to the sustenance of a desperate people.

Miriam represents the life force that drives us all. In the same way that we need water to live, we need to be able to rejoice in the miracles of life, singing and dancing when good things happen to us; but we also need to persevere in the difficult times, pressing on with life in the most dire of circumstances. These are the lessons that we, women and men alike, can learn from Miriam the Prophetess.

The *Mem* card represents **leadership.** As a small child, Miriam recognized her own definition of justice and stood up for her family's rights, thus making the best of a bad situation and ultimately helping to resolve it. We all have an element of leadership within us, even as small children. The key is to recognize our potential and claim it.

Whether it's leading people in song during a difficult time or providing the equivalent of much-needed water in the desert, there's always a way to take charge and help improve the lives of others. Use this card to meditate on the ways in which you could better realize your leadership potential in any aspect of your life.

14

נ
Nun

נח
Noach
(Noah)

These are the generations of Noah—Noah was a righteous man, perfect in his generations; Noah walked with God.

Genesis 6:9

Ten generations existed between Adam and Eve and Noah—yet by the time his story begins to be told in the Bible, society hasn't advanced very far. The world has quickly evolved into a sorry state of affairs, as people are known for stealing, cheating, and being violent and sexually immoral. But Noah was righteous, so when God decided that the entire world needed to be destroyed through an enormous flood and then re-created all over again, He saved only Noah and his family.

Much has been said about the qualification "in his generations." Some say that it means Noah was the only truly good person in all ten generations of existence. Others say that it's less positive: Noah may have been good compared to all of his neighbors, but put him in a different time and place, and he wouldn't have been described in the same way. One interpretation makes the comparison of a silver coin amid a pot of copper coins: Compared to the copper coins, the silver shines, but put the silver next to a gold coin, and there's no mistaking which one is more valuable.

Noah differs from other great figures in biblical history in that he doesn't question or argue with God. When God comes to him and says that He intends to destroy the whole evil world but will save him and his family through the ark, Noah doesn't ask why, nor does he try to change God's mind or stop the destruction from happening. Instead, he takes down the exact measurements and instructions on how to build the ark and how many animals to take with him, and he prepares himself to do as he's told.

In contrast, years later, Abraham will be told that the city of Sodom will be destroyed because of the immorality that existed there, and he'll bargain with God, trying to at least save the few good people who lived among the bad. Noah's silence here is just as controversial as his description of being righteous "in his generations." On the one hand, he's obedient and full of faith in the will of God; on the other, he doesn't exert the human will and ability to negotiate, interpret, and speak for oneself with which he was endowed at birth, and this is a disappointment.

It's always difficult to know when to be strong and silent and when to get up and fight for your case, especially when situations call for one and not the other. Whether or not Noah approached his circumstances "correctly" is not the issue—the important thing to know is that he "walked with God," he lived his life with a sense of purpose, knowing that there was a higher force guiding his life. This was what separated him from the rest of his society, making him worthy of the ark and of being the father of the new generations, the new beginning for the world.

Once the flood abated and the world began to function again, God made a covenant with Noah. He sent a rainbow in the sky and promised to never destroy the world at such a total capacity ever again. In turn, he established what we now know as the Noahide Laws, the seven guidelines for moral behavior that came long before the Ten Commandments.

These laws (do not murder, do not commit idolatry, do not steal, do not commit incest, do not cut meat from a living animal, do not be blasphemous, and do not bear false witness in court) apply to all of humanity, regardless of age, race, or religion. The fact that our basic laws of moral behavior are named after Noah tells us something very important: Being righteous, even if there will be others in future generations who will far exceed our righteousness, is worthy of creating a whole new world.

The *Nun* card comes to teach us the **Spiritual Theory of Relativity:** *Everything* is relative. We see things one way, based on our life experiences, but others with their different experiences see the opposite point of view.

Right and wrong are subjective categories that change all the time.

Although we cannot stand for injustice, and we must all strive to maintain the most basic principles of morality and fairness, we cannot entirely judge others according to our own standards.

Noah wasn't perfect, we're not perfect, and the world we live in isn't perfect. This card asks that you accept yourself and then look for ways to improve your behavior. Accept the world, but don't sit by and wait for it to fall apart when you can be active and help make it a better place.

A blind man can't be expected to paint landscapes of a world he's never seen, so know that you can only judge yourself according to your own abilities and circumstances.

15

ס
Samech

הר סיני
Har Sinai
(Mount Sinai)

On the third day when it was morning, there was thunder and lightning and a heavy cloud on the mountain, and the sound of the shofar [ram's horn] was very powerful, and the entire people that were in the camp shuddered. Moses brought the people forth from the camp toward God, and they stood at the bottom of a mountain. All of Mount Sinai was smoking because God had descended upon it in the fire; its smoke ascended like the smoke of a furnace, and the entire mountain shuddered exceedingly. The sound of the shofar grew continually much stronger; Moses would speak, and God would respond to him with a voice.

Exodus 19:16–19

Imagine being there at Sinai: Hundreds of thousands of people, slaves until just a few months before, are gathered together at the foot of a mountain in the desert—and smoke, fire, thunder, lightning, and the sound of the *shofar* blasting all lead up to the overwhelmingly awesome sound of the voice of God. How do you think this experience would make you feel?

Legend has it that only the first two of the Ten Commandments were given directly by God, and the last eight had to come through Moses. The people were too overwhelmed by their first direct access to God to handle the situation—so, since they were familiar with his voice and it intimidated them less, they begged Moses to speak instead. (Although, as Bible scholars point out, every individual heard God's voice differently, according to his or her own capacity and individual understanding, the direct experience of communication with the Divine proved to be more than they could handle.)

There's a tradition in Judaism that every single person in the world was at Sinai, and that those same souls have been reincarnated over and over again throughout the generations, even until today. That's why this scene of the first mass Revelation in history is so compelling to us even now. There's something in our souls that connects us to this event, remembers the fear that accompanied the excitement, and recognizes that in our most original state of being, we experienced it firsthand.

The *Samech* is shaped like a circle, and it represents protection and safety. Although on some level they're terrified, the people at Mt. Sinai also sense (though perhaps only subconsciously), that they're going to be fine. When Moses hears their cries and takes over the enunciation of God's words, the people are able to shield themselves from the frightening and foreign experience and take comfort in the familiar voice of their leader.

Only once the sound shifts from the mighty, ethereal voice of God to the human one of Moses are the people truly able to comprehend the deeper meaning of the Revelation. Like a perfectly round wedding ring, the experience of Sinai is binding and limitless at the same time, extending to every generation through endless reincarnations. Although the people now have concrete rules and regulations, and have accepted upon themselves the responsibility to live accordingly—which might seem like a burden—they've also been guaranteed the ultimate protection and guidance of their God. As if they're inside a metaphoric *Samech,* the people are now safely bound within the guidelines of their society, comforted by the permanence of it all.

❦ ❦

The *Samech* is your key symbol of **safety and protection.** Whether you're in a place of transition or going about your daily routines without interruption, you may now and then feel like a lost lamb, unsure of your place in the world.

Even when good things happen, we tend to question them and their place in the "bigger picture" of our lives. But the *Samech* reminds us that we're always enclosed within the protective embrace of a higher force.

Conjure up the experience of Sinai: Hear the foreign voice from above changing your reality day by day. You can conquer your fears and anxieties and quell your pride by focusing on the energy of the *Samech*.

Remember that everything is part of the universal circle of life. The experience you have today leads to the one you'll have tomorrow and so forth throughout lifetimes, and everything is just as it should be.

16

ע
Ayin

עקדת יצחק
Akedat Yitzchak
(The Binding of Isaac)

Then Isaac spoke to Abraham his father and said, "Father..." And he said, "Here I am, my son." And he said, "Here are the fire and the wood, but where is the lamb for the offering?" And Abraham said, "God will seek out for Himself the lamb for the offering, my son." And the two of them went together. They arrived at the place of which God had spoken to him; Abraham built the altar there, and arranged the wood; he bound Isaac, his son, and he placed him on the altar atop the wood.

Genesis 22:7-9

Most of the interpretations regarding the Binding of Isaac focus on the actions of Abraham, who had been previously tested nine times by God and who's considered the hero of the story. Because he was able to pass this final test, willingly preparing himself to sacrifice his beloved son (who was born when he was 100 years old and his wife was 90, after many years of infertility and struggle), Abraham is considered the paradigm of faith, willing to give up everything he'd lived for in order to fulfill the word of God.

Of course, this is one of the most morally problematic stories of the Bible, and generations of philosophers have struggled with whether Abraham succeeded or failed as a person regarding his willingness to kill an innocent man who was also his son. But whether or not this was an act of pure faith or a mistake, in the end Isaac wasn't destined to die, and God stopped Abraham from actually slaughtering his son seconds before the act was accomplished. The test was to evaluate Abraham's devotion, to prove to the world that he was a man willing to do anything and everything for his God.

But what of Isaac? He was 37 years old when this happened, hardly an ignorant child. Why isn't this considered to be a test of *Isaac's* faith rather than his father's? After all, being willing to sacrifice your own life is surely as significant as being willing to take the life of another.

Commentators say that when Abraham, Isaac, and their two servants set out on the morning of the Binding, only Abraham knew the true nature of their outing. But as they approached the mountain, Abraham saw a cloud signaling the presence of God, and soon Isaac did, too. The other two men didn't see the cloud, so Abraham asked them to wait below with the donkey while father and son ascended to the spot where the sacrifice was to be made—understanding that he and Isaac were on a different spiritual level than the other two.

In the dialogue above, which takes place as they walk up the mountain, Isaac comes to realize what's truly going to happen. He knows that the presence of the cloud implies a holy intention, and he knows that if he and his father were truly going to sacrifice a lamb, they'd need the animal in hand to do so. And as Abraham implies that God will provide the lamb, his son fully understands that *he* is the one who's meant to die on the altar. Even so, Isaac continues walking with his father, and he allows himself to be bound.

As a 37-year-old man, he would have been easily able to run away or overpower his ederly father, yet Isaac complies with this situation completely, willingly helping his father fulfill their destiny. Just as Isaac possessed the ability to see the holy cloud of God, he was also able to see into the future, and he knew that his legacy would not end that day on the mountain.

Isaac was able to comply because he had as much faith (though of a different sort) as his father. This is why the Binding wasn't as much of a "test" for Isaac as it was for his father. Abraham believed that he was going to have to kill his son, and the test was to see if he'd go ahead with it, despite his love for Isaac. But Isaac knew in the deepest parts of himself that this was only a test—he wasn't destined to become a martyr.

The Hebrew word *Ayin* means "eye." And the letter represents not just sight, but spiritual insight, the ability to "see" beyond the black-and-white details of the moment to the larger picture.

Later in his life, Isaac goes blind. Some say that the process began here, when the tears of his father and of the angels above fell into his own eyes—just before God stopped Abraham's hand from bringing the knife to his son's throat. Whatever the source of Isaac's blindness, it's significant that the forefather who's connected most to sight literally cannot see by the later years of his life. In other words, Isaac teaches us that the most important things to recognize in life are the things we can only see inside.

❧ ❧

The *Ayin* card comes to you in times of trial and questioning. We're all tested in various ways each and every day, and we must find ways to pass those tests and trust our **insight.**

In order to become a kabalist, you must learn to develop and trust your sixth sense and to see the light even in the darkness. This is the light that Isaac notices when he lies bound on an altar, and it's the same light he perceives when his eyes no longer function.

Trust what you see, both inside and out. Others may not be able to witness the cloud of glory or to understand the complexities of our daily trials, but that doesn't mean that they don't exist.

17

פ
Peh

פרעה
Pharaoh

And the Pharaoh's heart was hardened and he did not let the Children of Israel go…

Exodus 9:35

The story of the Jews' Exodus from Egypt is one of the most poignant tales of freedom in all of human history. Their harsh ruler, the Pharaoh, refuses to let them leave the country despite a series of plagues that the God of the Hebrews sends upon him. After every plague descends—blood, frogs, lice, swarms of wild beasts, epidemic, boils, hail, locusts, and complete darkness—Moses turns to the Pharaoh and asks him to "let my people go."

Nine times out of ten, the Pharaoh nearly relents, but at the last minute he "hardens his heart" and refuses. Only when the Plague of the Firstborn is carried out and the eldest son of every Egyptian household, including the Pharaoh's, is killed at midnight, does he finally give in and tell Moses to take the people and all their belongings and leave.

Throughout history we've seen what evil the human heart is capable of—from the Pharaoh to Adolf Hitler to Osama bin Laden, there have been people who do things most of us cannot even fathom. Nevertheless, those people do exist, and they teach us a lesson: Sometimes we have to see the worst in life before we can start rising up again to create a better world.

We also see this, to a lesser extent, in our own lives. Sometimes we must sink to our lowest levels of behavior before we start to improve. Addicts, for example, often need a near-death experience to compel them toward rehabilitation; and people who are grieving for a personal loss must often experience a deep sense of depression before they can begin the healing process. The same thing happened to the Pharaoh—he needed to experience the harshest personal tragedy (the loss of his son) in order to recognize how many children had already died at his hand.

Peh is the word for "mouth" in Hebrew. Spelled the same way, but with a different pronunciation (*"poh"*), the word also means "here." These two words and concepts are integrally linked: To speak is to be present, to be in the moment and consciously communicative. The Pharaoh needed to open his heart in order to open his mouth and give permission to let the people go—he needed to speak from the place of experience, from the present, from "here."

There's a famous rabbinic legend that says that when babies are in their mothers' wombs, they're endowed with all the knowledge in the world. When they're born, however, an angel taps them on the upper lip, creating the indent there underneath the nose, and they instantly forget everything. The process of life, then, is one of slowly re-learning and remembering things that we knew from the very start of our lives.

The Pharaoh also needed to go through a process of reconnecting with his lost humanity, finally accepting the fact that he wasn't an immortal god, but was subject to plagues just like every other Egyptian. And when he finally did come to realize this, to rediscover some of his inner morality, he was able to harness the power of speech (a distinctly human quality) to let the Jews go.

The *Peh* represents the incredible **power of speech** in our lives. Speaking is the catalyst for all action, and for any significant change in the world. To use our mouths, the ability that separates us from other life forms, is to be at our most powerful.

Look carefully at the shape of the *Peh*: Inside the black lines that form the letter, in the white space, there is a *Bet*. The *Bet*, as we've seen, is the first letter of the Torah, but it also represents looking at things from different angles. That the two letters are mystically intertwined teaches us a great lesson: Before we open our mouths to speak, we need to consider the bigger picture. Knowing that there's always another layer of truth to consider will help us communicate most effectively in life.

We say that "actions speak louder than words," but sometimes only words can lead us to profound action.

This card encourages you to soften your heart, open your mouth, and reclaim the knowledge that was given to you before you took your first breath. When you've accomplished those things, you can change the world.

18

צ
Tzaddik

צלם אלוהים
Tzelem Elohim
(In the Image of God)

So God created man in His image, in the image of God He created him; male and female He created them.

Genesis 1:27

This is the first of two descriptions given in Genesis for the creation of humankind at the beginning of the world. In the second (Gen. 2:18ff), man is created first, and then God forms woman by taking a piece of the man's "side" (the Hebrew word is *tzela*, traditionally translated as "rib") and creating a whole new being. In this original description, however, man and woman are created at one time. Some say that they're created as a single body, and later each "side" is separated from the other to produce the two individual people we know as Adam and Eve. Others say that they were created as separate bodies, but simultaneously and with completely equal status.

Whichever of the two versions of the human-creation story you choose to believe, what's essential to understand is that humanity was created in the Image of God *(be'tzelem Elohim)*, and that means that men and women have a purpose on this earth unlike any other creature formed in the first week of existence. Humankind was designed not just to be fruitful and multiply, as every animal is, but to dominate over nature and to explore their inherent powers. What separates us from the plants and animals is that we have within us a spark of Divinity that, if we're lucky, we can train ourselves to see and develop.

Trying to access that part of ourselves that's Godlike, the part that strives to make the world a better place and improve our personal traits, is the essential act of Kabala. By working toward recognizing our original holiness, our connection to the Divine source of creation, we begin to journey toward *Tikkun Olam* (the Healing of the World), which is the ultimate goal of our lives.

A *Tzaddik* is a righteous person, someone who makes it a priority to bring good things into the world, to give charity, and to give of themselves. You become a *Tzaddik* by first and foremost learning to connect with the fact that you were created *Be'tzelem,* in the Image. Once you internalize the fact that you contain within you an essential holiness, a purpose in life, you'll begin to see that everyone else also has this spark.

You cannot mistreat people—or be racist, judgmental, or cruel to your fellow human beings—if you truly believe that each and every one of us is created in the image of holiness.

To understand that the first person was actually a single man/woman unit, and that every person in the whole of history stems from this original being, is to understand that we're all truly created equal. Not only must we treat others with respect, we must also learn to treat *ourselves* with respect, striving to heal the often-ruptured world within ourselves as well as the outside world.

The *Tzaddik* helps to boost **self-confidence.** In times of doubt, when we question our personal values and take a cold, hard look at our lives in search of a deeper purpose, it's crucial to remember our origins: We're all made in the Image, we're all righteous people, or *Tzaddikim*.

Your body itself is holy, just as your soul is. Treat yourself with respect, as you would any holy object: Eat well, breathe, sleep, meditate, be creative, do good for the less fortunate. Only once you can relate to yourself as unique and holy will you truly see others the same way.

It is said that saving one life is like saving the entire world, and killing one person is like destroying the planet. This stems from the idea that in the beginning there was only one person who contained the most vital spark of life that will exist in every person throughout history.

Remember that we're all linked together in this world, and we're all crucial to its survival. Without any one of us, the world would be incomplete.

19

ק
Kuf

קן צפור
Kan-Tzippor
(Bird's Nest)

If a bird's nest happens to be before you on the road, on any tree, or on the ground—young birds or eggs—and the mother is roosting on the young birds or the eggs, you shall not take the mother with the young. You shall surely send away the mother and take the young for yourself, so that it will be good for you and will prolong your days.

Deuteronomy 22:6-7

This passage is one of 18 laws concerning the protecting of animals in the Bible. Among others, the Bible instructs us not to boil a kid in its mother's milk (which has evolved over time into the Jewish concept of *kashrut,* a system in which meat and milk are not to be eaten together at all), not to kill a mother and her offspring on the same day, and to help lift up an animal that may have collapsed from exhaustion on the road.

Although humans are given dominion over the animals in Genesis, we're also given the responsibility to care for and treat them as fellow creations of God. This tension between our accountability toward animals and our power over them is the source of many difficult questions. But what's clear from this passage is that we must first and foremost be sensitive to the nature of those that are consumed or otherwise used for our purposes.

By sending away the mother bird before taking her eggs or chicks, we accomplish several things: (1) We take into consideration the fact that animals are attached to their young and will suffer if they're separated from them—so by sending the bird away, she won't see her eggs taken, and the blow will be softened; (2) by not taking the bird along with her eggs as food, we help to preserve the species, ensuring that the breeding animal survives (environmentalists call this "sustainability"); (3) by exerting our responsibility toward animals before our power over them, we remind ourselves what's more important; and (4) we set an example of compassion for our own lives.

Now if sending away the mother bird is so important that it will lead to a long life for the one who performs the deed, just think how important it is to treat other people with such sensitivity. The emotional, practical, philosophical, and personal implications of this commandment are stunning: In performing (or merely understanding) such a small act, we can help ease the pain of the world, preserve the earth, put our power into place, and deepen our capacity for compassion and kindness to others.

The *Kuf* is first and foremost a letter of *kedusha*, holiness. The verb *lekadesh* means "to sanctify" or "make holy," suggesting that holiness is something to be actively achieved.

Look at how the letter itself is shaped: The character reaches down below the line as if descending into the "lower world" of earth from the "higher world" of spirituality. This teaches us that we can sanctify our lives, and infuse our existence with meaning and purpose, by seeking to elevate our daily actions and by having the consciousness of a higher purpose behind everything we do.

The *Kuf* card is a signal of **compassion.** Look beyond the surface of your actions and consider the fact that as humans, we're not all that matters in this world. The principle of kindness to animals teaches us the great lesson of being kind to *everyone,* from helpless infants to victims of crime to homeless families to the elderly.

Take a moment to envision the mother bird and her eggs. Put yourself in her position and consider her animal perspective. Now use your gift of human reasoning and power to perform an act of holiness.

20

ר
Resh

רבקה
Rivka
(Rebecca)

And when the time came for [Rebecca] to give birth, behold! There were twins in her womb. The first one emerged red, entirely like a hairy mantle; so they named him Esau. After that his brother emerged with his hand grasping on to the heel of Esau; so he called his name Jacob.... The lads grew up and Esau became one who knows hunting, a man of the field; but Jacob was a wholesome man, abiding in tents. Isaac loved Esau for he ate of his venison, but Rebecca loved Jacob.

Genesis 25:24-28

The matriarch Rebecca is one of the most highly developed female characters in the Bible, and she's also one of the most powerful.

Discovered at a young age by Abraham's servant Eliezer, she's recognized immediately as the destined mate for Isaac. Because of her intuitive kindness, Rebecca draws water for Eliezer and his camels before even being asked—for this, Eliezer offers to bring her back to Canaan to become the wife of Isaac. She immediately accepts and leaves her home, even though she's barely out of childhood and has never met Isaac.

The one characteristic that follows Rebecca throughout her life is her amazing sense of clarity. From the moment she sees Eliezer, she knows what to do; and when she first sees Isaac in the distance, after a long journey, she immediately senses who he is—not just another stranger encountered along the way, but her life partner.

After she and Isaac are married, Rebecca is barren for 20 years. When she finally does conceive, she has a difficult pregnancy and seeks out the reason for her troubles. She asks God directly why she's in so much pain, and He replies that she's carrying twins who are at war with one another even in the womb. This rivalry, she's told, will last as long as they live, but in the end the younger twin will triumph over the older one. Rebecca will keep this information to herself for years, but ultimately it will guide her behavior as a mother and become the basis for her future actions.

As the boys grow up, Esau, the elder, becomes a brute of a man, interested in hunting, women, and food; whereas Jacob, the younger, is more domesticated, bookish, and kind. Rebecca knows that although Isaac favors Esau, Jacob is the one who is destined to be the next in line spiritually; so when her husband is ready to pass on the blessing of the firstborn, which holds enormous spiritual power, Rebecca creates an elaborate scheme that changes history. She convinces Jacob to lie to his blind father, dress up in Esau's clothing, bring him venison as his brother would, and trick Isaac into giving him the blessing that will establish him as the dominant patriarch of his generation.

We're told that Rebecca does this not just because she favors one son over the other, but because she knows in no uncertain terms what *should* happen—that is, what is fair and right according to the prophecy she's received. Rebecca does all she can to actively change destiny, to act with confidence and ensure that Jacob is blessed. In this way, she makes sure that the prophecy she hears when she's pregnant is fulfilled, and that the line of righteous men continues with Jacob.

The letter *Resh* represents the *rosh,* the head. Rebecca is able to think logically and clearly and come up with solid, useful plans to do what's best for her family. After she secures the birthright for Jacob, she is able to see that Esau is violent enough to potentially kill his brother when he finds out what has happened, and she devises a plan in which Jacob goes to live with her brother Laban (where, incidentally, he will meet his future wives, Rachel and Leah).

Although her circumstances are difficult and she has to play one son against the other and deceive her husband, Rebecca knows with complete certainty what needs to happen in order for everyone to fulfill their true destiny.

※※

The *Resh* comes to those in need of **clarity**. Life is confusing, and often many paths compete for the taking. There is often more than one way to go, but from time to time we need to make definite, binding decisions.

Clarity need not be achieved only through prophecy—you can gain the ultimate knowledge all by yourself. But however you attain it, once something is clear in your mind, in the front of your consciousness, be careful not to waver from it.

Learn from Rebecca that you can change what seems to be set in stone. Your lot in life need not be the one given to you at birth—you need only be sure of yourself, and you can become whatever you need to be.

21

ש
Shin

שמע ישראל
Shema Yisrael
(Hear, O Israel)

Hear, O Israel: The Lord is our God, The Lord is One.

Deuteronomy 6:4

This single line, *Shema Yisrael, Adonai Eloheinu, Adonai Echad,* is considered the cornerstone of Jewish faith. The first prayer taught to young children and the last prayer recited on one's deathbed, in its simplicity and brevity this line captures the ultimate lessons of life: God is One, we are One, everything is Oneness. Described throughout the ages as the ultimate meditation tool and declaration of faith, the *Shema,* as it is known, is one of the most important sentences in the world.

Before the Jews finally enter the Land of Israel after 40 years of wandering in the desert, Moses recaps their experiences since the Exodus. He recounts the revelation at Mount Sinai and the giving of the Ten Commandments, and then proceeds to explain those commandments in preparation for living in a world where they will be relevant. In the midst of this he utters the *Shema,* followed by the instructions: "You shall love the Lord, your God, with all your heart, with all your soul, and with all your resources" (Deut. 6:5).

What we learn from this is that faith is not just a matter of belief but of totality. To believe is to feel it on every level—emotional, spiritual, practical, and even physical (the *Shema* is inscribed in the scrolls kept inside *mezuzahs,* traditional ornaments affixed to the doorposts of homes).

In order to really say the *Shema,* you have to be convinced of it on every level. In fact, if you look at the Hebrew text as it is written on a Torah scroll, you'll see that the last letters of both the first word and the last word of the sentence—*Ayin* and *Dalet*—are written twice as big as the other letters in the line. When you put the *Ayin* of *Shema* and the *Dalet* of

Echad together, you get the word *Ayd,* which means "Witness." Only if you are truly a witness to something can you fully comprehend it. And to truly *hear* what this prayer is about, you must witness its power for yourself.

The *Shin* is the first letter of the words *Shalom* ("peace") and *Shalem* ("complete" or "whole"), so to feel like a complete person is to be at peace with oneself. To feel the wholeness of the universe—the single life force that propels all of us and the world around us—is to also find peace, to hear the lessons of the universe explained.

Traditionally, this prayer is said sitting down, with one's eyes closed and the right hand covering them. Each word should be said slowly and focused on, one at a time. Doing this blind meditation teaches us to slow down, to minimize, to block out all outside interference, and to recognize that everything comes down to the single, original source of energy and light. In other words, despite our diverse backgrounds, we all come from the same place. When we truly recognize that unity is the goal of all life, that reconnecting with our origins is essential, we will have achieved wholeness.

The *Shin* is the beacon of **peace and wholeness.** By focusing on the *Shema* meditation, you can truly connect with the Oneness that is central to Kabala. Hear the lesson and make the statement true for yourself.

Realize that in the end, we all come from the same source. Close your eyes and focus on the light of creation . . . know that you are part of that light—we all are. You can find peace when you truly accept this principle and witness it for yourself.

22

ת
Tav

תהו ובהו
Tohu U'Vohu
(Vast Nothingness)*

In the beginning God created the heavens and the earth. Now the earth was a vast nothingness, with darkness upon the surface of the deep, and the Divine Presence hovered upon the surface of the waters. And God said, "Let there be light," and there was light.

Genesis 1:1–3

---

*The words *Tohu U'Vohu* have no clear literal English translation. The phrase has been rendered as "astonishingly empty," "unformed and void," "formless and empty," and "horrendous emptiness," among others. "Vast nothingness" is our original translation.

Have you ever wondered what the world was like before there was a world? How did the trees get here, or the mountains, or the sea? In every religion, there are myths and stories to explain the creation of the world, and in science there is the theory of evolution as well, but no one can ever know for sure how we came into existence.

In this passage, the explanation is as follows: In the beginning of time there was simply nothing at all. There was a void, a black hole, stillness . . . and then God decided to start something new—to create a world and populate it, and to see what we might do with it.

In Kabala, this nothingness is called *Ein Sof* ("Without End") and is considered to be another name for God. According to the Zohar, in the beginning there was only God—and still today there is only God because we're all made up of tiny fragments of His being, even though we have our own form. Kabalists believe that the state of nothingness, of primordial chaos, is a state that lasts throughout eternity. When we die our bodies become, in a sense, the same nothingness—we disintegrate and become formless and empty, just like the

Tohu U'Vohu that existed before there was a world in which our souls could be clothed in bodies. And so we go through an endless cycle of "nothingness" and "being" from life to life, throughout eternity.

If there is one thing we learn from the Torah, it is that there are no clear beginnings or endings to any story. Historical accounts reverberate in the present day, and single letters can change the way a whole book is read. Even in the first lines of Genesis we see that the mystery is profound and eternal. Notice that in Verse 2, there is a mention of water, but water was only created on the second day. Or was it? We don't know. This is to teach us to question assumptions and take nothing for granted.

Chaos will become order because that is the natural tendency of the world, just as the vast nothingness turned into an enormous universe filled with amazing creations. But in order to make sense of the senseless, to make order out of chaos, we have to put our energy into understanding it all, questioning and rethinking all of our assumptions.

The *Tav* is the last letter of the aleph-bet and the first letter of the word *Torah*. Torah is the beginning of knowledge, the first explanation for life and human action, the first family and national saga. The end, therefore, is nothing but a beginning. We know by now that this is true: The end of nothingness is existence, and the end of existence is nothingness—and the completion of every stage in life leads us to the next stage. Global creation and the creation of ourselves are both eternal processes.

The *Tav* comes to balance the *Aleph*. Although it also comes at the beginning of a new stage or the end of an old one, the *Tav* asks us to consider the uncertainty at hand rather than the solution or action to be taken. **Chaos** and **order** are part of the same process, and each are necessary to the other.

This card encourages you to meditate on the vast nothingness, the emptiness of a world before there is night and day, light and darkness, earth and sea. Remember, we're all part of this mystical state of mind, so let go of your assumptions and your earthly perspective. Allow yourself to experience the chaos of transition before you turn your energy toward the next stage of your life.

The end is only the beginning.

Bibliography

Books and Articles

Berg, Michael. *Becoming Like God: Kabbalah and Our Ultimate Destiny* (Kabbalah Publishing, 2004).

Elkins, Dov Peretz. *The Bible's Top 50 Ideas: The Essential Concepts Everyone Should Know* (Specialist Press International, 2005).

Green, Arthur. *Ehyeh: A Kabbalah for Tomorrow* (Jewish Lights, 2003).

Greenberg, Irving. "Living in the Image of God," published on the Internet at **www.beliefnet.com/story/12/story_1225_1.html**.

Heschel, Abraham Joshua. *The Sabbath* (Farrar, Straus & Giroux, 1951).

Kushner, Lawrence. *The Book of Letters: A Mystical Alef-Bait* (Jewish Lights, 1990).

_____. *The Way Into Jewish Mystical Tradition* (Jewish Lights, 2001).

Leibowitz, Nehama. *Studies in Bereshit (Genesis) in the Context of Ancient and Modern Jewish Commentary* (World Zionist Organization, 1981).

Matt, Daniel C. *The Essential Kabbalah: The Heart of Jewish Mysticism* (HarperCollins, 1995).

_____. *Zohar: The Book of Enlightenment* (Paulist Press, 1983).

Rubin, Gary. "Overcoming Destiny," published on the Internet at **www.myjewishlearning.com/ texts/Weekly_Torah_Commentary/toldot_ ujafedny5762.htm**

Steinsaltz, Adin. *Biblical Images* (Jason Aronson, 1994).

Their, Ela. "Letting Pharaoh Go: A Biblical Study of Internalized Oppression," in *The Women's Passover Companion,* ed. Rabbi Sharon Cohen Anisfeld, et al. (Jewish Lights Publishing, 2003). 246–250.

Zornberg, Avivah Gottlieb. *The Beginning of Desire: Reflections on Genesis* (Doubleday, 1995).

_____. *The Particulars of Rapture: Reflections on Exodus* (Doubleday, 2001).

Websites

www.beliefnet.com
www.geocities.com/m_yericho/ravKook/
   VAYIK64.htm
www.hir.org/torah/rabbi/parshiyot58.htm
www.inner.org
www.kabala.com
www.kabbalah.info
www.myjewishlearning.com
www.torah.org

Note: Translations from the Bible are taken in large part from *The Chumash: The Stone Edition* (Mesorah Publications, Ltd., 1993). When this translation was not to our liking, we consulted the Jewish Publication Society translation, and in some cases translated the passages ourselves.

About the Authors

Deepak Chopra has written more than 40 books, which have become international bestsellers and classics of their kind. Dr. Chopra is the Founder of the Chopra Center at La Costa Resort and Spa in Carlsbad, California and New York City. Websites: **www.intentblog.com** and **www.chopra.com**.

Michael "Zappy" Zapolin frequently delivers lectures to celebrities, business leaders, and politicians on how to use the Kabala's energies for fulfillment, success, and personal growth. His Website, **www.Kabala.com**, has received millions of visitors.

Alys R. Yablon is a freelance writer and book editor. Her Website is **www.alysablon.com**.

Notes